A CONCISE SUMMARY OF **DANIEL H. PINK'S**

To Sell Is Human

...in 30 minutes

A 30 MINUTE EXPERT SUMMARY

GARAMOND
— P R E S S —

CONTENTS

INTRODUCTION

Overview

In *To Sell Is Human: The Surprising Truth About Moving Others*, author Daniel H. Pink draws on social science to redefine the rules of selling, offering counterintuitive insights on how and why the art of the deal has changed. Pink contends that the line between seller and customer has blurred, and everyone, no matter the occupation, spends most of his or her time selling something—an idea, an agenda, an item—to somebody.

"Selling . . . is more urgent, more important, and, in its own sweet way, more beautiful than we realize. The ability to move others to exchange what they have for what we have is crucial to our survival and happiness. It has helped our species evolve, lifted our living standards, and enhanced our daily lives. The capacity to sell isn't some unnatural adaptation to the merciless world of commerce. . . . Selling is fundamentally human."

– Daniel H. Pink, *To Sell Is Human*

As technology reshapes how people work, buyers, who were once dependent upon salespeople for information, are often more informed than the salesperson. Even in a world where bargaining power has achieved parity, Pink argues that sales is not dead, but exists in a revised form he calls *non-sales selling,* the act of moving people to do something other than reach for their wallets.

With the new economy relying so heavily on non-sales selling, it is critical to be successful at it, which requires learning the new rules for moving others.

In Part One: Rebirth of a Salesman (Chapters 1–3), Pink argues for a broad rethinking of sales, laying the groundwork for a necessary shift in how sales is perceived in the second decade of the twenty-first century. In Part Two: How to Be (Chapters 4–6), Pink teaches readers the three qualities most valuable in today's sales– and non-sales–selling environment. According to Pink, the sales trade adage "Always Be Closing" has been replaced with the new ABCs—Attunement, Buoyancy, and Clarity. In Part Three: What to Do (Chapters 7–9), Pink concludes with three integral skills to hone in order to more effectively move others: pitch, improvise, and serve.

In *To Sell Is Human*, Pink's objective is not only to teach readers how to become more effective sellers, but also to shed new light on the act of selling, an act, he says, that is fundamentally human.

About the Author

Daniel H. Pink is an acclaimed expert on the art and science of motivation. His two *New York Times* best sellers, *Drive: The Surprising Truth About What Motivates Us* and *A Whole New Mind: Why Right-Brainers Will Rule the Future*, have sold more than a million copies and have been translated into thirty-three languages. Pink's 2009 TED talk on the science of motivation revolutionized long-held perceptions about intuitive thinking; it is one of the top twenty most-viewed TED videos of all time. In 2011, Thinkers50 named Pink one of the fifty most influential management thinkers in the world. His articles have appeared in the *New York Times*, the *Harvard Business Review*, *Fast Company*, and *Wired*. A graduate of Yale Law School, Pink served as an aide to Secretary of

Labor Robert Reich, and later as chief speechwriter for Vice President Al Gore. Pink lives in Washington, DC.

How the Book Came About

Following the thread of his previous business bestsellers, Daniel H. Pink approaches the history and practice of sales from the context of our rapidly changing culture and workplace in his 2012 publication, *To Sell Is Human.* In the introduction, Pink says the idea for the book was born out of a review of his own work calendar, noticing that most of his time was spent trying to persuade people to do something or to part with resources. "I am a salesman," Pink writes. "But most of what I do doesn't directly make a cash register ring." Neither does much of what others do in sales, Pink concludes. Sales have been redefined by technology, shifting industry, education, and emerging fields, and this book gives a snapshot of how the changing tide of traditional sales can be applied to non-sales selling—and vice versa—and what skills are required to do so successfully.

1

WE'RE ALL IN SALES NOW

Overview

In this age of technology, the traditional salesperson, personified by the Fuller Brush Man or the Avon Lady of yesteryear, is superfluous. Keystrokes and smartphones have rendered salespeople irrelevant, yet sales remains the second-largest occupational category. While one in nine workers performs traditional sales, the other eight perform *non-sales selling*—persuading, influencing, and convincing others in ways that don't involve anyone making a purchase—and they don't even know it. With this new data at hand, Pink concludes that there has not been a death of a salesman but a rebirth of an entire generation of sellers. "Because the salesperson is us," says Pink.

Chapter Summary

In Chapter 1, Pink introduces readers to the very last Fuller Brush Man in America, seventy-five-year-old Norman Hall, who was still selling door-to-door in the business district of San Francisco at the time of the book's publication. The iconic Fuller Brush Man is a relic of the days when door-to-door peddlers played a viable role in the country's sales force. Fuller Brush at its heyday in the 1960s was the equivalent of a billion-dollar business, but as the anecdote of Norman Hall illustrates, the market for door-to-door sales is gone, and online research and purchasing make middleman salespeople unnecessary. Yet although the Fuller Brush Man, with his dapper bow tie and satchel of goods, belongs to a past era, the author argues that the only thing obsolete about sales in today's society is an antiquated definition of selling.

To support this argument, Pink identifies a new sector of sales dominating the second decade of the twenty-first century, which he calls non-sales selling. Conventionally speaking, producing and consuming have been viewed as the most critical behaviors in economics, but Pink says much of what people set out to do these days is to *move* others—to influence or persuade them—to vote, invest, pay attention, or even date. From Facebook and Twitter to KickStart campaigns and Match.com to board meetings and budget proposals, non-sales selling consumes the personal and work lives of the majority of the population.

The Rise of Non-Sales Selling

Non-sales selling has escaped detection in formal surveys by the government. Although everyone from doctors and coaches to authors and craftspeople attempt to persuade others as part of their work, the statistical records of the US Bureau of Labor do not track non-sales selling. According to Pink, the work of moving others does not appear in federal labor statistics because the kinds of questions used in the surveys of workers are not the right kinds of questions. By conducting his own survey of about seven thousand US workers called *What Do You Do at Work?* Pink, assisted by an analytics group, found that across a professional spectrum, people working full time spend roughly twenty-four out of every sixty minutes involved in persuasion that does not result in a purchase. Further, the survey revealed that people considered this persuasive effort critical to the success of their work—something most workers believe they should be doing more of.

In this sense, Pink suggests, everyone is in sales even without full awareness—one in nine Americans works in sales, but the new data reveals that so do the other eight in nine. So the Fuller Brush Man is alive as new sales memes are sought and set. With the majority of Americans' livelihood dependent on the ability to move others, and do it well, it's time for a fresh look at the art and science of selling, beginning with answering the question: How did so many people get into the moving business?

Chapter 1: Key Points

- Technological advances reframed the conventional definition of sales work from a financial transaction for a good or service to the ability to persuade, influence, convince, and engage—an act the author calls moving others, or *non-sales selling*.

- As the basis for his analysis of the new face of sales, Pink devised a statistical tool called the *What Do You Do at Work?* survey, which polled seven thousand American workers and uncovered that eight in nine workers are involved in non-sales selling.

- Unbeknownst to the majority of today's workers, the salesperson is not obsolete, but very much alive in the form of non-sales selling.

2

ENTREPRENEURSHIP, ELASTICITY, AND ED-MED

Overview

As Pink explores the reasons for the workplace transformation, he identifies three factors that contribute greatly to the rise in the number of non-sales sellers: entrepreneurship, elasticity, and *Ed-Med*. While technology was expected to obliterate the need for salespeople, it has actually created an opening for small entrepreneurs to enter the workforce, which has turned most people into sellers.

Chapter Summary

Entrepreneurial businesses along with the shrinking budgets of large corporations create demand for non-specialized workers—those who wear many hats, of which sales is only one. While these smaller businesses and more amorphous job titles at large companies proliferate, the fastest-growing sector of work is Ed-Med, Pink's coined term for education and health services, where moving others is the key task to get the job done.

Entrepreneurship

Free-agent selling entities with no employees or with only a tiny staff, known as entrepreneurs, now make up most of the businesses in the United States and represent a growing sector. Economists predict that entrepreneurial business models represent the future of employment for the American middle class. Presently, being a seller on eBay provides significant income to about three-quarters of a million people in the United States. The free-agent business model is expected to skyrocket with the proliferation of smartphones—literally handheld minicomputers—which allow entrepreneurs to take credit card payments on their phones, essentially keeping shop wherever they are. So rather than eliminating salespeople as predicted, the author concludes, that technology has made more people into salespeople.

Elasticity

In contrast to the old model of large organizations where work was segmented and each person did just one thing or a set list of things, the no-employee businesses, or companies with only a few workers, demand that each person possess skills-based elasticity, the ability to do many things, including sales. Fierce competition and unpredictable market conditions over the past decade have even forced larger companies to adopt this model in order to remain profitable. The Palantir software company in Palo Alto, California, for example, sends computer scientists into the field to work with customers, requiring engineers to communicate and create solutions on the spot. The engineers are not taught how to sell but how to empathize the needs of the user and improvise. Although this is not direct sales, the interactions between customer and engineers do influence sales—indirectly and effectively. "As elasticity of skills becomes more common, one particular category of skill it seems always to encompass is moving others," Pink elaborates. An inventor can launch a business built around her invention, but beyond the engineering of the product, she must convince a bank for a loan, write a proposal for a grant, or convince prospective employees to accept a lower salary until profits start coming in, and on and on. In every aspect of the inventor's business, she is moving someone in a way that doesn't literally move her product out of the warehouse.

Pink stresses that the act of non-sales selling does not discriminate when it comes to the hierarchies in bureaucracies. Even those at the top of the org chart find themselves spending most of their time moving others, even in the form of motivating those who report to them to produce or accomplish things effectively.

Ed-Med

The largest job sector in the United States, as well as the fastest-growing sector in the rest of the world, is education and health services—or what the author calls Ed-Med. The author considers everyone from college professors to test-prep companies and from genetic counselors to registered nurses members of this skyrocketing sector. While historically the Ed-Med sector has been linked to caring and compassion, the author claims it is presently more closely aligned with the tough world of sales, but specifically of non-sales selling; from doctors to teachers, for workers in the Ed-Med sector to succeed, they must be able to move others to give up old behaviors and ideas in exchange for new ones.

Pink concludes that, with the dramatic and continuing growth of Ed-Med, the need for elasticity, and entrepreneurial business sectors, everyone has inadvertently ended up in sales, but because of the less-than-stellar reputation of selling, many begrudge this reality. Therefore, the author further posits, to expand their elasticity and progress effectively as non-sales selling people, they need first to overcome some outdated stereotypes about salespeople and negative judgments about sales in general.

Chapter 2: Key Points

- The transformation of workers into non-sales sellers can be linked to the increase in entrepreneurship, the demand for on-the-job elasticity, and the dominance of the *Ed-Med* job sector.

- Elasticity defines the ever-flexing skill set required in today's business—from entrepreneurial start-ups to small business to large corporations.

- Ed-Med (education and health services) is the largest-growing work sector and relies almost exclusively on the ability to move others.

- Sales carries a seamy reputation that causes those in the business of moving others to be unwilling to accept the new reality—that their livelihood depends on selling.

- The keys to accepting one's role of non-sales seller are debunking old sales stereotypes and letting go of obsolete characteristics and methods of selling.

3

FROM *CAVEAT EMPTOR* TO CAVEAT *VENDITOR*

Overview

Historically, sellers possessed all the information, leaving buyers at their mercy. This *information asymmetry* inspired the warning *caveat emptor*—buyer beware. It also led to deep mistrust of salespeople, who were negatively stereotyped. Now the Internet can arm buyers with more information than a salesperson, teacher, or doctor possesses. This leads to *information symmetry,* in which buyers now come fully informed to a sales transaction, so *caveat venditor*—"seller beware—has refashioned most encounters that involve moving others. This information symmetry has actually changed the way traditional sales is conducted, ironically appealing to the sensibilities of non-sales selling.

Chapter Summary

Many people resist the idea of being a salesperson due to prevailing negative impressions. A common attitude toward sales and salespeople is one of mistrust. In his *What Do You Do at Work?* survey, Pink discovered that the negative images people associate with sales are represented by the stereotypical used-car salesman, a figure distasteful because he represents deceit. The author argues that this lingering prejudice against sales as a profession is not only inaccurate but also outdated, because the marketplace has changed so radically—from *caveat emptor* (buyer beware) to *caveat venditor* (seller beware).

Caveat emptor was the marketplace precaution in former times when, in order to make a significant purchase such as a car, buyers had to endure what economics professor George Akerlof in 1967 dubbed "an asymmetry in available information," in which the seller had all the information and the buyer was largely in the dark. Thanks to the Internet, the warning in the marketplace has become *caveat venditor,* because both parties have the same access to information. As the balance of power has shifted, the sleaze factor has greatly diminished. In present times there is no reason for anyone to fear salespeople, even a used-car salesman; while a few sleazy operators may still be playing by the old rules, they are far outsold by honest dealers who are mastering the new rules of sales: no haggling, trust-based relationships, and transparency based on information symmetry leading to equal bargaining power on both sides. As an example of this, Pink points to CarMax, a successful used-car business, where salespeople make the same commission whether they sell a Mercedes or a Ford, so there is no need for deceit or pushiness, or for buyers to beware of an upsell that they can't afford or do not want.

The same information asymmetry that existed in the market also existed in education and health services, where the power was with teachers and health professionals, who were the gatekeepers of information. But the power here has shifted, too. As the Ed-Med sector grows in leaps and bounds, it will be necessary for practitioners to grow and change also, engaging their students or patients as critical partners in their own education or care. Moving others is a key ability in that realm as it never was before.

To master non-sales selling in changing times, the author insists people let go of perceptions made obsolete in this era of information symmetry, including the idea that salespeople are deceitful, money-grubbing blockheads with a natural-born propensity for sales. There are no "natural" salespeople, Pink urges, because all humans possess the selling instinct. The remainder of the book is dedicated to debunking these persistent myths and examining the elements of non-sales selling, so anyone can master the fundamentals of moving others.

Chapter 3: Key Points

- Selling, for many, conjures negative images that the author says are outdated and obsolete.

- *Information symmetry* is responsible for the new sales paradigm, where neither the seller nor the buyer is held at any disadvantage.

- The balance of power has shifted in sales from *caveat emptor* (buyer beware) to *caveat venditor* (seller beware), where honesty, fairness, and transparency are often the only viable path.

ATTUNEMENT

Overview

"Always Be Closing." This cornerstone of the sales cathedral, often referred to as the ABCs, has been rewritten by the author as the new ABCs of moving others: *attunement, buoyancy,* and *clarity*. In Chapter 4, Pink defines and examines the skill of attunement—the ability to connect harmoniously with others—by its three governing principles: increase your power by reducing it, use your head as much as your heart, and mimic strategically. Research shows that it is the person with a balanced personality, known as the ambivert, who can most effectively master attunement and is therefore the most successful at moving people.

Chapter Summary

During the heyday of information asymmetry, the motto of predatory salesmanship was "Always Be Closing," or ABC. But the era of relentless-pressure selling is over, no longer effective in these times of information symmetry. Pink offers a new ABC of sales, conveying the three essential qualities useful in moving others: attunement, buoyancy, and clarity. This chapter deals with attunement, defined as the ability to harmonize actions and perspectives with those of others in a given context—to see from others' perspectives. This attunement, or *perspective-taking*, follows three key principles: (1) Increase your power by reducing it; (2) Use your head as much as your heart; and (3) Mimic strategically.

1. *Increase your power by reducing it.* A sense of power blocks attunement. To be skillful at perspective-taking, it's necessary to assume the position of less or no power, since the best perspective-takers—according to social science research—are those with inferior status. By taking on a lower-status position in an encounter, sellers are more apt to see others' viewpoints and be in a position to move them.

2. *Use your head as much as your heart.* Initiating encounters with an assumption of having less power is a cerebral rather than an emotional skill, as perspective-taking is not the same thing as feeling empathy. Perspective-taking may be used in tandem with empathy, but the cognitive act of perspective-taking has been proven to be the more effective of the two. Having empathy, though, is handy in building enduring relationships and defusing conflicts. Someone skilled at this second principle of attunement recognizes that people are not solo units but are connected by relationships to others in specific contexts, which can activate a seller's *social cartography*—the ability to "size up" or "read" a group or a person and adjust one's style accordingly, a strong example of being attuned.

3. *Mimic strategically.* Attunement with others is deepened by the physical acts of mimicry and touch. Because humans are quicker to trust those who resemble themselves, subtle mimicry has been shown effective in achieving trust, and thus attunement. Mimicry of manner and vocal patterns are cues that communicate understanding and reduce the emotional distance between people. If mimicry is not performed deftly, however, and people become aware of it, they will turn wary. Studies have shown that a light touch placed on the forearm of a customer during a verbal exchange increases effectiveness in sales transactions.

The Ambivert Advantage

Despite the common presumption that extroverts make the best salespeople, there is scant evidence to support the claim. In fact, neither extroverts nor introverts are the most successful at moving others. Research shows that ambiverts, those in the middle of the personality spectrum, are best at sales—whether traditional or non-sales selling—because they respond to others in a balanced way, knowing when to put forth and when to hold back. Personality test scores indicate that most people are ambiverts; Pink argues that this fact supports his premise that all people, to some extent, are born to sell.

Chapter 4: Key Points

- According to Pink, the new ABCs of non-sales selling are: *attunement, buoyancy*, and *clarity.*

- To master attunement sellers should: (1) increase their power by reducing it; (2) use their head as much as their heart; and (3) mimic strategically.

- The most attuned, and therefore the most successful salespeople are ambiverts, those who are neither too shy nor too outgoing, and know when to engage others and when to hold back. According to research, most people fall into the ambivert category, which supports the author's theory that "to sell is human."

5

BUOYANCY

Overview

In the art of moving others, the second quality one cannot do without is buoyancy, whether in traditional sales or non-sales selling. Buoyancy is the ability to keep oneself from sinking when rejections and setbacks feel oceanic. In this chapter, Pink returns to the last Fuller Brush Man as an example of a buoyant seller, and examines the sociological research about three constructive behaviors that comprise this condition of remaining unsinkable: interrogative (as opposed to declarative) self-talk, maintaining an appropriate positivity ratio (not pure Pollyannaism), and using an optimistic explanatory style for things that do not go as planned.

Chapter Summary

Norman Hall, the last Fuller Brush Man in America, is a model of buoyancy when things don't go his way. As defined by Pink, buoyancy is that quality that keeps one above water when failure and rejection threaten to sink the spirit. Hall, who in his forty years of door-to-door sales has met with uncounted rejections, and whose efforts have met diminishing returns in the Internet age, keeps going because he possesses buoyancy.

Buoyancy has three components, according to Pink. The first is self-talk, which is used when preparing to undertake the work of moving another person. But contrary to conventional business wisdom, it is not declarative self-assertions taught in sales training courses that work, which intonate a cheerleader tone, e.g., "You can do this!" The most effective kind of self-talk, says Pink, is the interrogative sort, which poses the question, "Can I make this sale?" Researchers have found that *interrogative self-talk* is measurably more effective than bold assertions, such as "I will succeed!" or "I am the best salesperson on the planet." To the brain, assertions create pressure, whereas questions imply choices. Those who phrase their self-talk as a question are more likely to succeed, research shows, because the brain responds to questions not only by shifting emotions but also by offering strategies for achieving the task suggested in the question.

The second component of buoyancy is *positivity in proper balance.* For example, Hall approaches each day expecting some negativity but organizes each day to include more interactions he knows will be positive. Studies show that positivity is a powerful tool, but an excess of positivity results in unhealthy outcomes. Research by Barbara Fredrickson and Marcial Losada showed that positive emotions enhance creativity, intuition, and options for behavior. However, blocking all negativity is not healthy, and will render one clueless and self-delusional, void of the ability to self-improve. Studies show the ideal ratio of positive to negative emotion is three to one—that is, as the Pink explains, "for every three instances of feeling gratitude, interest, or contentment, they experienced only one instance of anger, guilt, or embarrassment."

Buoyancy's third and final component is an *optimistic explanatory style,* a kind of self-talk that comes after the act of moving others is complete. When Hall meets rejection during his sales calls, the way in which he explains it to himself is a key aspect of his success. For example, he might tell himself the person was having a bad day, or that he or she was having a cash-flow problem. Successful salespeople optimistically see rejections as temporary, and do not take them personally. Studies have shown that optimism is a powerful catalyst for persistence and keeps people moving forward. But optimism should not ignore what is real and true about a situation. The ideal form of optimism, according to Martin Seligman, one of the originators of positive psychology, is "flexible optimism—optimism with its eyes open."

Chapter 5: Key Points

- The second facet of the ABCs of moving others is buoyancy, the ability to stay afloat amid a sea of rejection and bad news.

- Buoyancy is achieved through *interrogative self-talk*, *positivity in proper balance*, and an *optimistic explanatory style* in response to rejection. Interrogative self-talk poses questions that challenge a person to find answers, and is preferred over declarative self-talk such as "I'm good at this."

- Positivity is the second key to achieving buoyancy; however, there is such a thing as too much positivity. A positive-negative ratio of three to one has been shown to lead to the most buoyancy.

- An optimistic explanatory style explains failures in a non-personal way, and is the third and final pathway to buoyancy.

CLARITY

Overview

Clarity, the third and final quality of the ABCs of moving others, is a mind-set uniquely valuable to the new era of non-sales selling; it allows one to see people and situations in fresh and more revealing ways. Clarity replaces traditional problem solving with the more versatile skill of problem finding. Clarity requires that people move more slowly in thinking and allows the client to be served with a creative and fresh approach to situations. Clarity can be achieved by invoking the use of contrast, because things are better understood when people see them in comparison with other things, as opposed to viewing them in isolation. Contrast can be effectively achieved through providing any five important framing devices: the less frame, the experience frame, the label frame, the blemished frame, and the potential frame.

Chapter Summary

Clarity is the third essential quality required for moving others, expressed as a cognitive predisposition to see others and see situations from fresh and revealing perspectives. Clarity seeks to identify problems rather than simply solve problems, to examine things in innovative ways. For example, Pink describes how clarity was applied successfully to the longstanding issue of people not saving enough for their retirement years.

The conventional problem-solving approaches by government and social scientists to encourage more saving fell short in one way or another until social psychologist Hal Hershfield, exhibiting clarity, uncovered a previously unknown problem: people felt an emotional disconnection between their present and future selves. So Hershfield showed some study participants computer-generated avatars of themselves as wrinkled old people, which they were required to look at for a certain period of time before answering a survey. In the survey, those who were shown avatars of their older selves allocated twice the amount of money others allocated toward savings for old age. Hirschfield had identified the real problem: emotional distance between people and their future selves impedes a clear picture of the reality of a situation. Having the clarity to find a hidden problem helps people face issues more effectively, and positions them to better move others.

Problem finding makes a salesperson valuable because it supports clarity. To confused buyers, clarity is a valuable service and can enhance a seller's ability to move others.

The clarity to be a problem finder involves creativity and flexible thinking, and it takes a bit longer than conventional problem solving. Before technology brought information symmetry, salespeople were all problem solvers because they had the information the buyer needed to solve a problem. In present times, buyers can find their own information to solve problems; so the role of the salesperson becomes valuable when the person needs help finding the correct problem to solve. In this new age, effective salespeople brainstorm, problem find, offer insights, and help discover new opportunities. According to Pink, salespeople were once successful because they could access information; now they need to ask good questions and act as "curators" of information.

Research shows that clarity depends on contrast and so the art of moving others includes the ability to frame options for others, a principle that Robert Cialdini, the Arizona State University scholar and one of the most important social scientists of the last generation, calls "the contrast principle." One of Cialdini's core insights is that contrast operates within, and often amplifies, every aspect of persuasion, which is why the most essential question one can ask is: "Compared to what?"

That question can be raised by framing an offering in ways that contrast with its alternatives and therefore clarify its virtues. The five techniques for framing include: *the less frame*, reducing the choices for those selecting a product; *the experience frame*, framing a sale experientially because people value experience over things; *the label frame*, carefully selecting a label because it influences behaviors; *the blemished frame*, including a small negative aspect following a list of positive ones; and *the potential frame*, which emphasizes future performance over past performance, because people have more faith in the unknown of potential.

An extension of framing is providing an "off-ramp," which the author defines as clear instructions for what people should do. The following chapters that comprise Part Three of the book offer readers such an off-ramp. Now that readers know how to be, thanks to Pink's ABCs of non-sales selling—attunement, buoyancy, and clarity—Pink shows readers what to do to most effectively move others.

Chapter 6: Key Points

- The third and final tenet of the ABCs of moving others is clarity, which Pink describes as the capacity to help others see their situations in fresh and more revealing ways and to identify problems they didn't realize they had.

- The way to best achieve clarity is to help buyers through a process of problem finding, replacing the problem solving that drove sales in the days of information asymmetry.

- Clarity relies on the "contrast principle," a useful concept that entails framing buyers' options using the following techniques: *the less frame, the experience frame, the label frame, the blemished frame,* and *the potential frame.*

- Clarity on how to think without clarity on how to act can leave people unmoved, so no matter the framing technique used, buyers must be provided an "off-ramp."

PITCH

Overview

The elevator pitch has been a standard in sales for more than a century. Once thought the most succinct form of moving others, it has become obsolete by the transforming workplace in which competition is fierce and attention spans have shortened. The traditional elevator speech has been replaced, according to Pink, by six new shorter alternative ways to influence others: the one-word pitch, the question pitch, the rhyming pitch, the subject-line pitch, the Twitter pitch, and the Pixar pitch. In this chapter the author identifies the form of each pitch, along with what works and what doesn't, according to current research.

Chapter Summary

Pitching is the ability to distill a point to its persuasive essence. The purpose of a pitch, according to a study published in the *Academy of Management Journal*, isn't to move others to immediately adopt one's ideas, but to begin a dialogue that leads to both parties' participation and arrival at an outcome that appeals to them both. When a party is invited in as a collaborator, more pitches are likely to be green-lighted. People are so bombarded with information now that they have shorter attention spans, and the old elevator speech has been replaced by six types of pitches: *the one-word pitch*, *the question pitch*, *the rhyming pitch*, *the subject-line pitch*, *the Twitter pitch*, and *the Pixar pitch.*

The One-Word Pitch. The one-word pitch attempts to make others think of the product when they hear one word. Pink says the one-word pitch pushes brevity to its breaking point. When most people hear the word "search" for example, they immediately think of Google. The ultimate goal of the one-word pitch is when anybody thinks of a company, they utter that word. When anybody utters that word, they think of the company.

The Question Pitch. Decades of research show that questions can be more powerful than statements in moving others. Although the wrong questions—those in which the foundational argument is weak—create a negative outcome, a well-crafted interrogative engages others to discover reasons for themselves why to agree or not agree to the question. In Reagan's political campaign against Carter, for example, his question pitch "Are you better off now than you were four years ago?" was successful; when Mitt Romney used the same pitch in his campaign against President Barack Obama in the 2012 election, it was not successful because the underlying argument was weak.

The Rhyming Pitch. The rhyming pitch is effective because rhyming enhances what scientists call *processing fluency,* the fluidity with which the mind makes sense of things. Further, studies show that people attribute greater accuracy to statements made in rhyme than the same facts expressed in non-rhyming sentences. This kind of pitch was employed by Johnnie Cochran, the attorney representing O. J. Simpson in his 1995 murder trial. After his client struggled to get his hand into a bloody glove found at the murder scene, Cochran pitched the jury with this rhyme: "If it doesn't fit, you must acquit."

The Subject-Line Pitch. E-mail subject lines are pitches in themselves, because they are pleas for attention or invitations to engage. Knowing how to write an effective subject line will enhance the effectiveness of the pitch. E-mails are viewed as most critical when the sender is more relevant. Studies also suggest people open an e-mail based on its usefulness or whether it piques curiosity. Lastly, the language used in an e-mail's subject line matters—the more specific, the better.

The Twitter Pitch. The Twitter pitch forces a 140-character message. To be successful, it must be engaging enough to get a response. Studies indicate that more than half of all tweets sent are not worth reading. The loser categories are: (1) complaints ("I missed my train."); (2) me now ("I'm about to cheat on my diet with death by chocolate."); and presence maintenance (generic, no-purpose hellos or other greetings, e.g., "Good night, all."). Winning tweets cause a recipient to further the conversation through asking questions, clicking links, and forwarding useful information.

The Pixar Pitch. Rooted in the appeal of storytelling made popular by Pixar Animation Studios, most famous for *Toy Story*, the Pixar pitch is a template of six sentences in narrative order: *Once upon a time_____. Every day _____. One day _____. Because of that _____. Because of that _____. Until finally _____.* This pitch works because stories are generally persuasive, and this one is structurally sound and succinct.

Chapter 7: Key Points

- The purpose of a pitch isn't to move others to adopt one's ideas immediately, but to begin a dialogue that leads to both parties' participation and arrival at an outcome that appeals to them both.

- The traditional elevator pitch is now obsolete because of changing times and technology, as well as shortened attention spans.

- Modern pitch making includes six shorter alternative ways to influence others: *the one-word pitch, the question pitch, the rhyming pitch, the subject-line pitch, the Twitter pitch,* and *the Pixar pitch.*

8

IMPROVISE

Overview

Improvisation is critical for anyone who wants to move others. Where salespeople were once trained to recite prepackaged language with the goal of closing a sale, now dynamic, complex, and unpredictable conditions that favor improvisation have replaced the static conditions of old. Improvising forces sellers to listen deeply in order to align themselves on the spot harmoniously with the customer. In an era of information equity, scripts are out the window; sales and non-sales selling now rely directly on skills used in improvisational theater—essentially three guiding behaviors: (1) *hear offers*; (2) *say, "Yes, and"*; and (3) *make your partner look good.*

Chapter Summary

Sales no longer means delivering a scripted message to overpower objections. In this age of information parity, good talking has been replaced by good listening, which can be learned from studying improvisational theater. Half a century ago, improvisation redefined theater, demanding of actors the ability to listen, observe, and create plot elements. Now salespeople need the same skills set.

Cathy Salit, a master trainer in Manhattan, teaches business people techniques of improvisation with the underlying goal of making them better listeners. The training is a whole-body endeavor, where participants must work in intimate proximity to others, observing body cues and taking personal risks. The point is to listen and be able to respond to not only the words heard but also to the non-verbal messages expressed in body language.

Hear Offers. Hear offers is a principle that hinges on attunement because its first rule requires close listening. In theater improvisation, where one actor must decide her next move based on the move made by her co-actor, Salit says that hearing offers means "to take in anything and everything someone says as an offer you can do something with." To hear an offer, one must be attuned to the other person, open to their perspective. This ability, according to Salit, demands slowing down and shutting up long enough to grasp that one does not listen for one thing or another, nor simply wait for one's turn to talk. Attuned listening allows people to hear offers and thus opportunities they might otherwise have missed. Pink describes an improvisation in which one actor grabs an invisible steering wheel and invites the listening actor to lock his door; the listening actor has been given an offer to sit in a vehicle, and on the spot creates details (what kind of vehicle, the purpose for the transportation) that will keep the story moving forward. The only way to hear offers in all of their shapes and sizes, suggests Pink, is to change the way one listens and then change the way one responds.

Say, "Yes, and." Say, "Yes, and" is a principle that depends on buoyancy, specifically the trait of positivity. The second rule of improvisational theater is to accept all offers with a "yes, and" response rather than a "yes, but" response. "Yes, and" is a form of positivity practice that allows progress to be achieved by helping people see the potential of an idea, and applies to the act of moving others. In any planning process, Pink explains, when suggestions are met with negativity, framed as "yes, but," the conversation spins and spins and no forward movement is made—the action stops. When responses are framed as positive solutions rather than objections, flow is maintained and creativity emerges, keeping the process spiraling upward toward possibility, instead of downward to futility.

Make Your Partner Look Good. Make your partner look good is a principle that enables clarity. Good improvisational actors know that making their fellow performer shine reflects equally on them and on the success of the scene. In the history of scripted and predatory sales, whether the customer looked good was not important; now it is critical to sales and non-sales selling success.

The act of making someone else look good facilitates learning the needs and motives of others, and with this clarity comes less of a power struggle and more of a win-win for all parties concerned.

Chapter 8: Key Points

- Sales and non-sales selling operate in an unpredictable and complex environment now, where the ability to recite pre-scripted arguments convincingly is no longer valuable.

- Moving others in the age of parity requires listening closely and using improvisational response techniques, which enable attunement, buoyancy, and clarity.

- The three rules of improvisation that lead to successful selling and non-sales selling are: (1) *hear offers* (attunement); (2) *say, "Yes, and"* (buoyancy); and (3) *make your partner look good* (clarity).

SERVE

Overview

The last thing to do to move others is to do it selflessly, and in service to the world. Moving others is not a money-grubbing undertaking because the ultimate purpose of sales and non-sales selling, according to the author, is to serve others and make the world better. Research shows that people work more effectively when they work in service to others, even strangers. Moving others can therefore make a significant and lasting contribution to the betterment of the world, the author posits, if two objectives are kept in mind: keep efforts personal and make them purposeful.

Chapter Summary

Evidence suggests that people produce their best work when they do it in service to others. Moving others, in some cases, can even save lives. Georgetown University economists James Habyarimana and William Jack used the practice of moving others as part of a method to reduce traffic deaths in Kenya, a country where the recklessness of *matatu* (bus) drivers contributed to the highest rates of traffic deaths in the world. In one group of *matatus*, stickers that encouraged riders to heckle the driver and to protest bad driving were placed in front of passengers. "Don't just sit there as he drives dangerously!" the sticker demanded.

"Stand up. Speak up. Now!" The stickers moved the passengers to change their behaviors; in those vehicles in which stickers were posted, there was more than a 50 percent reduction in insurance claims for *matatu* accidents resulting in injury or death.

According to Pink, service is much more than smiling at a customer during a purchase transaction; instead, it is acting in a way that improves the lives of others. This kind of service requires a twofold approach—to make service personal and purposeful.

Making service personal has been shown to improve performance in the health care field, where the outcomes directly impact the well-being of others. Yehonatan Turner, a radiologist in Israel, performed a study in which, after placing the photograph of patients on their relative X-rays, CT scans, or MRIs, increased empathy was reported by the radiologists and they were more meticulous in the way they examined the scans. The study measured incidental findings—where an X-ray of a broken bone, for example, reveals a tumor that the radiologist was not looking for but can be life saving. The study showed that when the patient's face did not appear on the scan, 80 percent of incidental findings went undetected.

Making service purposeful requires serving others for a reason that transcends personal gain. Businessman Robert Greenleaf in 1970 wrote a groundbreaking essay defining the servant-leader model, in which a leader made herself the servant of others by refraining from harming others, being a listener first, and being empathetic and accepting. This model caused a significant stir and was received as both threatening to the prevailing paradigm and inspiriting to those interested in an alternative to leading by force. The servant-leader model transformed the business world. Pink claims it's time to apply Greenleaf's philosophy to sales. *Servant selling,* or the servant-seller model, is the act of moving others. It is successful only if it results in improving the lives of those whom have been moved to do or to purchase something, and if the world is somehow a better place after the interaction is complete.

Service selling encapsulates the practice of moving others. Those who move others are creative and motivated by higher ideals, claims Pink, because they understand that selling is a naturally human act.

Chapter 9: Key Points

- Sales and non-sales selling are ultimately about service, not in the traditional variety of helping a customer make a purchase, but to better the world and conditions for other people.

- Moving people can achieve something greater than exchanging resources, but it requires making efforts personal and purposeful. When sellers treat work personally, they communicate to buyers that there is a person behind the product or service who cares about improving another's life; working purposefully communicates a motivation to improve the world.

- The final secret to moving others is the combination of personal and purposeful work that produces a service to others, something the author calls *servant selling*.

CONCLUSION

Traditionally it was believed that only some people were in sales. They set out to sell things and provide services, and their buyers relied on them. In this age of information symmetry, where the balance of power has equalized, the business world has been reshaped, calling for flexible skill sets and making sellers of almost everybody. Sales changed from a world of *caveat emptor* to *caveat venditor*. Pink says that because of this shift in the dynamics of sales, there needs to be a new set of sales rules, and offers his ABC of sales—attunement, buoyancy, and clarity. To master these ABCs, new skills need to be honed—the ability to pitch, to improvise, and to serve.

In place of the once ubiquitous elevator pitch, people now use six replacement pitches more suited to the shorter attention spans of the age of technology. Instead of following scripts and pushing a sale, people use improvisation to listen better and maintain positive forward movement. And rather than following self-centered goals, people move others as a service to improve their lives and to make the world a better place.

"Finally, at every opportunity you have to move
someone . . . be sure you can answer the two
questions at the core of genuine service.

1. If the person you're selling to agrees to buy,
will his or her life improve?

2. When your interaction is over, will the world be
a better place than when you began?

If the answer to either of these questions is no,
you're doing something wrong."

– Daniel H. Pink, *To Sell Is Human*

Lightning Source UK Ltd.
Milton Keynes UK
UKOW041106030413

208598UK00001B/190/P